# Updat

# Gout

# CookBook

# Series

# (Dinner)

Discover A New 20+ Gout friendly Dinner  For Reversing And
Healing Gouty Arthritis

# Mary J. Hart

# Table of content

# Grilled Salmon Salad with Quinoa

## Ingredients:

- 4 salmon filets
- 1 cup quinoa
- 2 cups vegetable stock
- 1 cucumber, diced
- 1 red ringer pepper, diced
- 1/4 cup red onion, finely cleaved
- 1/4 cup new parsley, cleaved
- 2 tablespoons lemon juice
- 2 tablespoons olive oil
- Salt and pepper to taste

## Instructions:

1. Flush the quinoa under cool water to eliminate any sharpness. Combine the vegetable broth and rinsed quinoa in a

saucepan. Cover and simmer for approximately 15 minutes, or until the quinoa is cooked and the liquid has been absorbed, before bringing to a boil. Set the quinoa aside to cool and fluff it with a fork.

2. The grill should be heated to medium-high.

3. Season the salmon filets with salt and pepper on the two sides.

4. Dice the cucumber and combine it with the red bell pepper, red onion, and fresh parsley in a bowl. Add the cooked quinoa to the bowl and throw to blend the fixings.

5. Whisk together the olive oil, salt, and pepper in a small bowl. Toss the quinoa salad with the dressing to evenly coat the ingredients.

6. Put the salmon filets on the preheated barbecue and cook for around 4-5 minutes for every side or until the salmon is cooked through and drops effectively with a fork.

7. After taking the salmon off the grill, allow it to rest for a few minutes.

8. The quinoa salad should go with the grilled salmon.

9. Partake in your flavorful gout-accommodating supper!

10. Preparation time: Around 30 minutes.

# Heated Chicken Bosom with Steamed Broccoli

### Ingredient:

- 4 chicken bosom filets
- 2 tablespoons olive oil
- 2 cloves garlic, minced
- 1 teaspoon dried thyme
- 1 teaspoon paprika
- Salt and pepper to taste
- 4 cups broccoli florets
- 2 tablespoons lemon juice

### Instructions :

1. Set the oven temperature to 200°C (400°F).

2. Olive oil should be drizzled over the chicken breast fillets before placing them in a baking dish.

3. Sprinkle minced garlic, dried thyme, paprika, salt, and pepper over the chicken, it are very much covered to ensure the two sides.

4. The chicken should be baked for about 20 to 25 minutes, or until the internal temperature reaches 165 degrees Fahrenheit (74 degrees Celsius).

5. Steam the broccoli florets until tender but still crisp while the chicken bakes. This can be accomplished by steaming the broccoli in a steamer basket or by boiling a small amount of water in a pot, adding it, and then covering the pot with a lid until it is cooked.

6. The baked chicken should rest for a few minutes after being taken out of the oven.

7. Press new lemon juice over the steamed broccoli.

8. Serve the steamed broccoli with the baked chicken breast.

9. Take pleasure in your tasty, gout-friendly meal!

10. Preparation time: 35mins

# Shrimp Stir-Fry with Brown Rice

## Ingredients

- 1 pound shrimp, stripped and deveined
- 2 tablespoons low-sodium soy sauce
- 1 tablespoon rice vinegar
- 1 tablespoon honey
- 1 tablespoon sesame oil
- 2 cloves garlic, minced
- 1-inch piece of ginger, ground
- 2 cups blended vegetables, (for example, chime peppers, broccoli, snap peas)
- 2 tablespoons vegetable oil
- 3 cups cooked earthy colored rice

**Instructions**:

1. Mix the honey, sesame oil, soy sauce, rice vinegar, minced garlic, and grated ginger in a small bowl. Place aside.

2. In a large skillet or wok, heat the vegetable oil to medium-high heat.

3. Add the blended vegetables to the skillet and sautéed food for 3-4 minutes until they begin to mellow yet are as yet fresh.

4. Add the shrimp to the opposite side of the skillet after moving the vegetables to one side. The shrimp should be cooked for two to three minutes on each side, turning opaque and pink.

5. Spread the shrimp and vegetables in the skillet with the prepared sauce. Cook for an additional 1-2 minutes,

stirring frequently to evenly coat everything.

6. Eliminate the skillet from intensity and serve the shrimp pan sear over cooked earthy colored rice.

7. Partake in your flavorful gout-accommodating supper!

8. Planning time: Around 25 minutes

# Vegetable Curry with Cauliflower Rice

## Ingredients :

- 1 can (14 ounces) of coconut milk 2 cups mixed vegetables (such as carrots, bell peppers, zucchini)
- 1 small head of cauliflower, grated into rice-like texture Fresh cilantro, chopped (for garnish)
- Salt and pepper to taste

## Instructions:

1. 1 tablespoon coconut oil 1 onion, diced 2 cloves garlic, minced
2. 1 inch piece of ginger, grated
3. 1 tablespoon curry powder
4. 1 teaspoon ground cumin
5. 1 teaspoon ground turmeric

6. 1 teaspoon paprika

7.

8. Heat the coconut oil in a large pot or skillet over medium heat.

9. Add the diced onion, minced garlic, and ground ginger to the skillet. Saute the onion for two to three minutes, or until it becomes translucent and fragrant.

10. Add the curry powder, ground cumin, turmeric, and paprika to the skillet. To evenly coat the spices and onions, thoroughly stir.

11. Add the coconut milk and diced tomatoes with their juices. Mix everything together with a spoon.

12. Incorporate the mixed vegetables into the curry sauce by stirring them into the skillet.

13. Cover the skillet and simmer for about 15 minutes, or until the vegetables are tender, at a low heat.

14. Grate the cauliflower with a box grater or pulse it in a food processor until it resembles rice while the curry is simmering.

15. In a different container, heat a limited quantity of coconut oil over medium intensity. Cook the rice made from grated cauliflower for 5 to 6 minutes, or until it becomes tender.

16. Salt and pepper the cauliflower rice according to taste.

17. Serve the cauliflower rice with the vegetable curry on top, and top it with some freshly chopped cilantro.

18. Take pleasure in your tasty, gout-friendly meal!

# Turkey Meatballs with Zucchini Noodles

**Ingredients** :

- The turkey meatball recipe:
- 1 pound ground turkey
- 1/4 cup almond flour
- 1/4 cup grated Parmesan cheese 1/4 cup fresh parsley chopped
- 1 beaten egg 2 minced cloves of garlic
- 1 teaspoon dried oregano 1/2 teaspoon salt 1/4 teaspoon black pepper
- 4 medium zucchini 2 tablespoons olive oil 2 minced garlic cloves Season with salt and pepper to taste

**Instructions**:

1. Preheat the broiler to 400°F (200°C). Use parchment paper to line a baking sheet.

2. In an enormous bowl, join the ground turkey, almond flour, ground Parmesan cheddar, cleaved parsley, beaten egg, minced garlic, dried oregano, salt, and dark pepper. Make sure all of the ingredients are thoroughly mixed in.

3. Shape the turkey combination into meatballs, around 1 to 1.5 crawls in width, and put them on the pre-arranged baking sheet.

4. Prepare the turkey meatballs in the preheated broiler for around 18-20 minutes or until they are cooked through and sautéed outwardly.

5. While the meatballs are heating up, set up the zucchini noodles. Utilize a spiralizer or a vegetable peeler to make long, dainty strips from the zucchini.

6. In a large skillet, heat olive oil to a medium temperature. Sauté the minced garlic for about one minute to release its aroma.

7. When the zucchini noodles are just tender, add them to the skillet and cook for two to three minutes, stirring occasionally. To taste, season with salt and pepper.

8. Over the zucchini noodles, serve the turkey meatballs. They can be topped with marinara sauce, grated Parmesan, and chopped fresh basil if you want to.

9. Partake in your flavorful gout-accommodating supper!
10. Planning time: Around forty minutes.

# Grilled Portobello Mushroom Burgers:

**Ingredients** :

- Four large Portobello mushroom caps;
- two tablespoons balsamic vinegar;
- two tablespoons olive oil;
- two minced cloves of garlic;
- one teaspoon dried thyme;
- salt and pepper to taste;
- four whole wheat burger buns;
- your choice of Gout-friendly toppings (such as lettuce, tomato, onion, and avocado).

**Instructions**:

1. Preheat the barbecue to medium intensity.

2. Mix the balsamic vinegar, olive oil, minced garlic, dried thyme, salt, and pepper in a small bowl.

3. Brush both sides of the Portobello mushroom caps with the prepared marinade after removing the stems.

4. Gill-side down, place the mushroom caps on the preheated grill. Each side should be cooked for 5 to 6 minutes, or until grill marks appear and the meat is tender.

5. Toast the burger buns on the grill until they are lightly browned and warmed through while the mushrooms are grilling.

6. Allow the grilled Portobello mushroom caps to cool for a minute after taking them off the grill.

7. Place each grilled mushroom cap on a toasted burger bun to make the mushroom burgers. Toppings that are good for gout, like avocado, lettuce, tomato, or onion, can be added.

8. With a side of salad or roasted vegetables, serve the burgers made with grilled Portobello mushrooms.

9. Partake in your delicious gout-accommodating supper!

10. Preparation time: Roughly 20 minutes.

# Quinoa Stuffed Bell Peppers

**Ingredients**:

- 4 bell peppers (any color)
- 1 cup cooked quinoa
- 1 cup black beans, rinsed and drained
- 1 cup diced tomatoes
- 1/2 cup corn kernels
- 1/2 cup diced onion
- 2 cloves garlic, minced
- 1 teaspoon ground cumin
- 1/2 teaspoon paprika
- 1/2 teaspoon dried oregano
- Salt and pepper to taste
- 1/2 cup shredded cheddar cheese (optional)
- Fresh cilantro, chopped (for garnish)

**Instructions**:

1. Preheat the oven to 375°F (190°C). Grease a baking dish with olive oil or line it with parchment paper.
2. Cut the tops off the bell peppers and remove the seeds and membranes. Set the bell peppers aside.
3. In a large skillet, heat some olive oil over medium heat. Add the diced onion and minced garlic, and sauté for 2-3 minutes until they become fragrant and softened.
4. Add the cooked quinoa, black beans, diced tomatoes, corn kernels, ground cumin, paprika, dried oregano, salt, and pepper to the skillet. Stir well to combine all the ingredients.
5. Cook the quinoa mixture for 5-7 minutes, allowing the flavors to meld

together. Adjust the seasoning if needed.

6. Stuff each bell pepper with the quinoa mixture, packing it tightly. Place the stuffed bell peppers in the prepared baking dish.

7. If desired, sprinkle shredded cheddar cheese over the stuffed bell peppers for added flavor.

8. Cover the baking dish with foil and bake in the preheated oven for about 25-30 minutes or until the bell peppers are tender and the filling is heated through.

9. Remove the foil and continue baking for an additional 5 minutes to allow the cheese to melt and lightly brown.

10. Remove the stuffed bell peppers from the oven and garnish with freshly chopped cilantro.

11. Serve the quinoa stuffed bell peppers as a flavorful gout-friendly dinner.

12. Preparation time: Approximately 50 minutes

# Quinoa Stuffed Bell Peppers

## Ingredients:

- 4 red bell peppers, any color;
- 1 cup cooked quinoa;
- 1 cup rinsed and drained black beans;
- 1 cup diced tomatoes; 1/2 cup corn kernels;
- 1/2 cup diced onion;
- 2 minced cloves of garlic;
- 1 teaspoon ground cumin;
- 1/2 teaspoon paprika;
- 1/2 teaspoon dried oregano; salt and pepper to taste;
- 1/2 cup shredded cheddar cheese; fresh cilantro chopped for garnish.

## Instructions :

1. Set the oven temperature to 375°F (190°C). Oil a baking dish with olive oil or line it with material paper.

2. Remove the seeds and membranes from the bell peppers by cutting off the tops. The bell peppers should be put away.

3. Olive oil can be heated in a large skillet over medium heat. Sauté the diced onion and minced garlic for two to three minutes, or until they become soft and fragrant.

4. The ground cumin, paprika, dried oregano, cooked quinoa, black beans, diced tomatoes, corn kernels, salt, and pepper should all be added to the skillet. Mix well to join every one of the fixings.

5. Allow the flavors to combine by cooking the quinoa mixture for 5-7 minutes. Change the flavoring if necessary.

6. Fill each bell pepper tightly with the quinoa mixture. Place the stuffed bell peppers in the baking dish that has been prepared.

7. Sprinkle the stuffed bell peppers with shredded cheddar cheese if you like for extra flavor.

8. Cover the baking dish with foil and bake for 25 to 30 minutes, or until the filling is heated through and the bell peppers are tender.

9. Bake for an additional 5 minutes after removing the foil to allow the cheese to melt and lightly brown.

10. Eliminate the stuffed chime peppers from the stove and topping with newly slashed cilantro.
11. The quinoa-stuffed bell peppers make a delicious dinner that is good for gout.
12. Preparation time: Roughly 50 minutes

# Grilled Salmon with a Lemon Dill Sauce

**Ingredients**:

- 4=salmon fillets,
- 2 tablespoons olive oil,
- 1 tablespoon lemon juice,
- 2 minced cloves of garlic,
- 1 teaspoon dried dill, salt and pepper to taste.
- 1/2 cup plain Greek yogurt
- 1 tablespoon lemon juice
- 1 tablespoon hacked new dill
- Salt and pepper to taste

**Instruction:**

1. The grill should be heated to medium-high.

2. To make a marinade for the salmon, combine the olive oil, lemon juice, minced garlic, dried dill, salt, and pepper in a small bowl.

3. Brush the salmon fillets evenly with the marinade before placing them in a shallow dish. For about 15 minutes, let them marinate.

4. While the salmon is marinating, set up the lemon dill sauce. Combine the plain Greek yogurt, lemon juice, chopped fresh dill, salt, and pepper in a separate bowl. Make sure all of the ingredients are thoroughly mixed in. Season the dish to your liking.

5. Place the marinated salmon fillets, skin side down, on the grill grates when the grill is heated. Close the barbecue and cook for around 4-5

minutes for each side, or until the salmon is cooked to your favored degree of doneness.

6. Eliminate the barbecued salmon filets from the barbecue and let them rest for a couple of moments.

7. The grilled salmon should be topped or served with a dollop of lemon dill sauce.

8. Take pleasure in your tasty, gout-friendly meal!

9. Preparations time: Approximately 30 minutes

# Quinoa and Roasted Vegetable Salad

## Ingredients:

- 1 cup quinoa,
- 2 cups water,
- 1 small eggplant, diced,
- 1 zucchini, diced,
- 1 red bell pepper, diced,
- 1 yellow bell pepper, diced,
- 1 small red onion, sliced,
- 2 tablespoons olive oil,
- 1 teaspoon dried oregano, salt and pepper to taste,
- 1/4 cup crumbled feta cheese.

## Instructions:

1. Preheat the broiler to 400°F (200°C). Use parchment paper to line a baking sheet.

2. The quinoa should be rinsed under cold water in a fine-mesh sieve. This aids in the removal of bitterness.

3. Bring the water to a boil in a saucepan. Add the washed quinoa and lessen the intensity to low. Cover the pan and simmer for approximately 15 minutes, or until the quinoa is cooked and all of the water has been absorbed. Cover it and let it sit for five minutes after turning off the heat. Cushion the quinoa with a fork and put it away.

4. In the mean time, spread the diced eggplant, diced zucchini, diced red chime pepper, diced yellow ringer pepper, and cut red onion on the

pre-arranged baking sheet. Sprinkle with salt and pepper, dried oregano, and olive oil. Toss to evenly coat the vegetables.

5. The vegetables should be roasted for 20 to 25 minutes in a preheated oven, or until they are tender and lightly browned. For even cooking, stir them once or twice during roasting.

6. In a huge blending bowl, consolidate the cooked quinoa and broiled vegetables. Throw delicately to combine everything as one.

7. Sprinkle the disintegrated feta cheddar over the quinoa and broiled vegetable blend. To evenly distribute the cheese, lightly toss.

8. Freshly chopped parsley should be added to the salad of quinoa and roasted vegetables.

9. Lemon wedges can be squeezed over the salad and served chilled or at room temperature.

10. Take pleasure in your tasty, gout-friendly meal!

11. Planning time: Around 40 minutes

# Lentil Curry with Cauliflower Rice

**Ingredient :**

- 1 cup dried lentils (any assortment), washed and depleted
- 1 tablespoon olive oil
- 1 little onion, diced
- 2 cloves garlic, minced
- 1 tablespoon curry powder
- 1 teaspoon ground cumin
- 1/2 teaspoon ground turmeric
- 1/4 teaspoon cayenne pepper (discretionary, acclimate to taste)
- 1 can (14 ounces) diced tomatoes
- 1 can (13.5 ounces) coconut milk
- 2 cups vegetable stock

- 1 little cauliflower head, ground or finely cleaved
- Salt and pepper to taste
- New cilantro, slashed (for decorate)

**Instructions :**

1. Heat the olive oil in a large pot over medium heat. Add the diced onion and minced garlic, and sauté for 2-3 minutes until they become fragrant and clear.

2. Add the curry powder, ground cumin, ground turmeric, and cayenne pepper (if utilizing) to the pot. Mix well to cover the onions and garlic with the flavors, and cook for one more moment.

3. Add the flushed and depleted lentils, diced tomatoes (counting the juice), coconut milk, and vegetable stock to

the pot. Mix everything together with a spoon.

4. Cover the pot and reduce the heat to low after the mixture reaches a boil. Allow it to stew for around 20-25 minutes or until the lentils are delicate and cooked through.

5. Grate or finely chop the head of cauliflower while you make the cauliflower rice.

6. In a different skillet, heat some olive oil over medium intensity. The cauliflower rice should be cooked in the skillet for about 5-7 minutes, stirring occasionally, until it is soft but not mushy. To taste, season with salt and pepper.

7. Season the lentil curry to taste with salt and pepper after the lentils have been cooked.

8. The lentil curry should be served with cauliflower rice on top.

9. Use freshly chopped cilantro to garnish.

10. Take pleasure in your tasty, gout-friendly meal!

11. Planning time: Around 45 minutes

# Stuffed Chicken Breast in the Greek

## Ingredients:

- 2 boneless, skinless chicken bosoms
- 1/2 cup spinach leaves, cleaved
- 1/4 cup disintegrated feta cheddar
- 1/4 cup diced tomatoes
- 1/4 cup diced red onion
- 2 tablespoons cleaved Kalamata olives
- 1 tablespoon cleaved new parsley
- 1 tablespoon olive oil
- 1 teaspoon dried oregano
- Salt and pepper to taste
- Lemon wedges (for serving)

## Instructions:

1. Preheat the broiler to 400°F (200°C). Oil a baking dish with olive oil or line it with material paper.

2. Butterfly each chicken breast with care using a sharp knife by cutting horizontally through the thickest part but not all the way through. Like a book, open the chicken breasts.

3. The chopped spinach, crumbled feta cheese, diced tomatoes, diced red onion, chopped Kalamata olives, chopped parsley, olive oil, dried oregano, salt, and pepper should all be combined in a bowl. Blend well to join every one of the fixings.

4. On one side of each butterflied chicken breast, spread the spinach and feta mixture. Fold the other side over to cover the filling.

5. Secure the stuffed chicken bosoms with toothpicks or kitchen twine if necessary to keep the filling set up.

6. Place the stuffed chicken bosoms in the pre-arranged baking dish. Olive oil can be drizzled all over the chicken breasts.

7. In a preheated oven, bake the chicken for about 25 to 30 minutes, or until it is cooked through and no longer pink in the middle.

8. The stuffed chicken breasts should rest for a few minutes after being removed from the oven.

9. Lemon wedges, which can be squeezed over the Greek-style stuffed chicken breasts, should be served on the side.

10. Take pleasure in your tasty, gout-friendly meal!

# Quinoa Stuffed Portobello Mushrooms

**Ingredients**:

- 4 huge Portobello mushrooms
- 1 cup cooked quinoa
- 1/2 cup hacked spinach
- 1/4 cup diced red chime pepper
- 1/4 cup diced red onion
- 2 cloves garlic, minced
- 2 tablespoons ground Parmesan cheddar
- 1 tablespoon olive oil
- 1 teaspoon dried thyme
- Salt and pepper to taste
- New basil leaves, hacked (for decorate)

**Instructions** :

1. Set the oven temperature to 375°F (190°C). Use parchment paper to line a baking sheet.

2. Eliminate the stems from the Portobello mushrooms and delicately scratch out the gills utilizing a spoon. Put the mushrooms on the baking sheet that has been prepared.

3. Olive oil should be heated in a skillet over medium heat. Add the minced garlic, diced red ringer pepper, and diced red onion. Sauté for 2-3 minutes until the vegetables are relaxed.

4. Cook the chopped spinach in the skillet for an additional 1-2 minutes, or until it begins to wilt.

5. Combine the cooked quinoa, sautéed vegetables, grated Parmesan, dried thyme, salt, and pepper in a mixing

bowl. To incorporate all of the ingredients, thoroughly stir.

6. Partition the quinoa stuffing uniformly among the Portobello mushrooms, pressing it firmly into the mushroom covers.

7. Place the stuffed Portobello mushrooms in the preheated broiler and prepare for around 20-25 minutes or until the mushrooms are delicate and the stuffing is warmed through.

8. The stuffed Portobello mushrooms should cool for a few minutes after being removed from the oven.

9. Decorate with newly hacked basil leaves.

10. Serve the quinoa stuffed Portobello mushrooms as a delectable gout-accommodating supper.

# Grilled Balsamic Chicken with Roasted Vegetables

## Ingredients:

- 4 boneless, skinless chicken breasts
- 1/4 cup balsamic vinegar
- 2 tablespoons olive oil
- 2 cloves garlic, minced
- 1 teaspoon dried rosemary
- 1/2 teaspoon dried thyme
- Salt and pepper to taste
- 2 zucchini, sliced
- 1 red bell pepper, sliced
- 1 yellow bell pepper, sliced
- 1 red onion, sliced
- 1 tablespoon olive oil
- 1/2 teaspoon dried oregano
- 1/2 teaspoon paprika

## Instructions:

1. In a small bowl, whisk together the balsamic vinegar, olive oil, minced garlic, dried rosemary, dried thyme, salt, and pepper to create a marinade for the chicken.

2. Place the chicken breasts in a shallow dish and pour the marinade over them. Make sure the chicken is evenly coated. Let it marinate in the refrigerator for at least 30 minutes or up to overnight.

3. Preheat the grill to medium-high heat.

4. In a separate bowl, toss the sliced zucchini, red bell pepper, yellow bell pepper, and red onion with olive oil, dried oregano, paprika, salt, and pepper.

5. Place the marinated chicken breasts on the preheated grill and cook for about 6-8 minutes per side, or until the internal temperature reaches 165°F (74°C) and the chicken is cooked through.

6. While the chicken is grilling, preheat the oven to 400°F (200°C). Spread the seasoned vegetables on a baking sheet and roast in the oven for about 20-25 minutes, or until the vegetables are tender and slightly caramelized.

7. Remove the grilled chicken from the heat and let it rest for a few minutes.

8. Serve the grilled balsamic chicken alongside the roasted vegetables.

9. Enjoy the flavorful gout-friendly dinner!

10. Preparation time: Approximately 50 minutes (including marinating time)

Printed in Great Britain
by Amazon

37583041R00030